T0122164

Leaving
the
Past Behind

Moving Forward for God

Peggy Clevenger

WESTBOW
PRESS®
A DIVISION OF THOMAS NELSON
& ZONDERVAN

THE HOLY BIBLE, NEW INTERNATIONAL VERSION®, NIV® Copyright © 1973, 1978, 1984, 2011 by Biblica, Inc.® Used by permission. All rights reserved worldwide.

This book is a work of non-fiction. Unless otherwise noted, the author and the publisher make no explicit guarantees as to the accuracy of the information contained in this book and in some cases, names of people and places have been altered to protect their privacy.

WestBow Press books may be ordered through booksellers or by contacting:

WestBow Press
A Division of Thomas Nelson & Zondervan
1663 Liberty Drive
Bloomington, IN 47403
www.westbowpress.com
1 (866) 928-1240

Because of the dynamic nature of the Internet, any web addresses or links contained in this book may have changed since publication and may no longer be valid. The views expressed in this work are solely those of the author and do not necessarily reflect the views of the publisher, and the publisher hereby disclaims any responsibility for them.

Any people depicted in stock imagery provided by Getty Images are models, and such images are being used for illustrative purposes only. Certain stock imagery © Getty Images.

ISBN: 978-1-9736-2619-0 (sc)
ISBN: 978-1-9736-2620-6 (e)

Library of Congress Control Number: 2018904627

Print information available on the last page.

WestBow Press rev. date: 04/12/2018

Contents

Preface

When I felt led by the Holy Spirit to write this piece, I grappled with just how to go about doing it. I knew it shouldn't be a tell-all, but I wanted to write it in a form that other women who are struggling to put their past behind them could relate to and begin living for God. Women like me. Women who in the past meandered through their young lives doing what felt good, living life with abandon. Women struggling with guilt and shame over things they did and said that could never be taken back and wouldn't be forgotten. I fervently prayed, "Dear Lord, give me the wisdom and words I need to help others." When Jesus promised the disciples that the Father would send a Counselor to be with those who loved Him, he said: "But the Counselor, the Holy Spirit, whom the Father will send in My name, will teach you all things and will remind you of everything I have said to you" (John 14:26, NIV). Praise God that I have the Holy Spirit to counsel me and give me the words that He would have me share with others.

Dearest friend, are you living under the mistaken belief that you can't be forgiven for things you've done? Do you throw your hands up in exasperation every time someone brings up the shameful things in your past? Do you watch in horror while your children make the same kinds of mistakes you made, knowing that they learned them from you? Do you live in fear that new friends will discover your sordid past and hate you for it? Now will you say a prayer that the Lord will open your eyes to His truth and give you peace?

A prayer for healing the heart:

Precious Lord, thank you for Your love and mercy! I've lived a life of sin for which I am feeling shame daily. I know that through my repentant confession to You the one who shed Your blood for me, that my sins have been forgiven. Help me to overcome my own crippling guilt so that I can serve You. As I read Your Word give me understanding and peace. Amen.

Leaving
the
Past Behind

Shadow of hand on wall Credit: dourleak

Going through the Motions and Reaching for the Light

This is the message we have heard from Him and declare to you: God is light; In Him here is no darkness at all. If we claim to have fellowship with Him yet walk in the darkness, we lie and do not live by the truth. But if we walk in the light, as He is in the light, we have fellowship with one another, and the blood of Jesus, His Son, purifies us from all sin.

—1 John 1:5, NIV

I like to sleep in complete darkness. This is almost impossible these days, even out in the country, because we have security lights. When I get up during the night, I don't want to turn the light on, knowing it will wake up my husband. I grope my way through the room, stubbing my toe as I try to find the door. After ramming into it with my forehead, I stumble to the kitchen and run my hand down the wall, trying to locate the light switch. When I find the switch and flick it on, the whole room is illuminated so brightly that it hurts my eyes, much like the pain I felt when I finally admitted that I was willingly stumbling in spiritual darkness.

As an older college student during a recent study session, I listened as a young woman extolled the wonders of her relationship with her boyfriend. She was clearly smitten with him as she explained breathlessly how excited she was to hear that her hero was soon returning from serving in the Middle East. She was full of adoration and anticipation. I asked her if they planned to marry. "No," she said, "he already has a wife." Without missing a beat, she went on to explain their plans to go away together for a long weekend as soon as he could get away. "But first," she said, "he needs to spend some time with his son, who has Asperger's syndrome." I sat in stunned silence as I realized that it wasn't the affair that shocked me, but the ease with which she could discuss it and her lack of concern that her boyfriend had not only a wife, but also a child who desperately needed him. I also realized how easy it was to explain away behavior that was less than noble or, as this woman did, just ignore the obvious. My face burned as I became more and more uncomfortable with the conversation. I was only too glad to break free from that group of women.

"Lord," I asked, "was I really that cold and unfeeling when I was her age? Did I really talk about my experiences as though the feelings of others didn't matter?" I knew the answer was a resounding *yes*. My feelings of shame over my past, and my pity for her, clung to me like a bug that wouldn't brush off, tenaciously stinging me until it raised a welt. The only balm for this pain was prayer. I thanked God for His willingness to show mercy and to forgive me.

Tugging at my heart was the knowledge that the world was full of women like me: women with pasts that haunt us and make us burn with shame. How many, I wondered, are out there regretting past acts and are willing to do anything to erase their mistakes, afraid God would not forgive them? The world is full of people who have had little if any moral or religious upbringing. Those of us who know better have even less excuse for our sins. The fact remains that God loves us all, and He wants everyone to turn away from sin and focus on Him.

When I was growing up, my church experience was sporadic. My precious grandmother saw to it that my mother and her children went to church during her visits with us. Dad wasn't at all interested in church and was very vocal about it. There was a period during my teen years when Grandma lived just down the street from us, and Mother really did try to go to church. But my bitter father had a way of making us all miserable over it. I think Mom just gave up. So my deep and abiding relationship with Christ did not begin until many years later.

I married in 1974, at the age of eighteen. It is obvious to me now that I was far too immature to be in a committed relationship and begin raising a family. *Now* I realize that only God can give the kind of love that would fill the empty hole in my heart. At that time, I was unable or unwilling to accept it. So I walked into a marriage lacking the one ingredient that would keep us focused and get us through the tough times.

After our son was born, we began attending church.

We went to Bible study and joined the choir. We truly were trying to do the right thing, but I was shocked to discover that my husband was not the man I had imagined he was. He wasn't perfect, and he had his own personal issues to deal with. Like many young people with unrealistic expectations, I was caught off guard and crushed to the core. It seemed that our relationship became unbearably awkward overnight. We tried counseling with our pastor, but the damage was done, and I chose to deal with the situation by rebelling against God's Word. I filed for divorce and began seeing someone else. Our children were five and six years old by this time, and the situation was intensely confusing and painful for them. At a time in my life when I should have only been *thinking* about marriage and starting a family, I was destroying my reputation and cutting off relationships with others who could have counseled me. I was also hurting the two people I loved most in the world: my children.

In retrospect, I realize that if my relationship with God had been more sincere and less superficial, our marriage would have been different. Yes, we attended Bible study and joined in philosophical conversations. We carried our Bibles and sang our hearts out on Sunday mornings. We took our children to Sunday school, but we were simply going through the motions of being Christians. I hadn't had the heart-changing experience that was available to me through Christ's suffering and death.

The man I was involved with was older and more experienced than I was. During that time, I went through a period of bitterness so intense that when I saw a happily married older couple, I told myself that it was all a sham. I determined there was no such thing as a "good and faithful marriage." I was bitter and disbelieving at anniversary announcements in the newspaper.

I had few female friends. Who wants to hang out with a bitter woman who has a chip on her shoulder and is looking to prove a point? The fact is that at the time, I just didn't care what others thought of me. I brought myself down so low that I finally was convinced that nothing and no one, not even God, could make my life better. I didn't think that I had a fighting chance to regain my integrity in other people's eyes—or even in my own mind.

I thought that if I moved away, I could "start over," meet new people, and have a new life. So I packed up my eleven- and thirteen-year-old children and moved them halfway across the country. I had a home built on a piece of land, and I began a new career. I soon found that simply relocating would not make me a different person. I began the same old habits with new people. The environment was different, but I was the same unhappy, bitter person.

The only decent thing I did in those days was care for my children. I loved them and went to the sports, dance classes, scouting, and school functions. They were the only sane and good things in my life, and I clung to them. I had done something good. I had brought two beautiful children into the world, and I was determined that they would have everything I could provide for them. God was good to my children while I was muddling through; He had His hand in everything they did. Even though I didn't ask for His help, He was there. I was just too stubborn and blind to recognize His presence.

I met Joe and ended the earlier relationship, but I was determined that I would not get married just to be hurt again.

I had convinced myself that there was no real happiness out there for me. I didn't want to get married, but I wanted all the perks that came with a committed relationship. When I look back on that time, I shake my head in wonder at how hypocritical and contradictory my attitude was. Today I ask myself, "What on earth was I thinking?"

I had turned away from the only hope I had and was stumbling around in the dark alone, not even knowing what it was I was looking for. At the height of my confusion, Joe noticed me. I had always been attracted to him, but now things were different. *He* started looking at me in a new way. I saw in him a good man, and I wanted him for myself. We got married, and a new chapter in my rocky journey began.

It wasn't until Joe and I had been married for eight years that we began to attend church together and became serious about serving God. But we had a whole lot of housecleaning to do before we would ever be useful servants for the Lord, starting with repentance and rededication. It wasn't easy to face up to our mistakes. The temptation to justify our behavior was ever present: "He said … she said … they did … so we did." There were only excuses—just excuses.

I realized that, like groping for a light switch in the dark, I had been slamming my head and stubbing my toe into everything and everyone I came in contact with. I had to face my own lack of integrity. I had to admit to myself that I had destroyed my reputation and that others looked at me with wariness. I walked through my days in a haze of self-accusation and fear of what lay ahead. What if I tried to befriend people and they turned their backs on me? I needed guidance and knew that any person I turned to might recoil at my story. I had to fall on my knees and beg God to help me.

Trying to build a Christian character with years of baggage hanging around my neck began with the miracle of God's love and forgiveness. Thinking that people might not trust me and might even hate me for who I was before was enough to make me quake at the mere thought of being in a Christian environment. Only with God's help was I able to make myself walk into a church and face others. I had to confess that I fell far short of where I ought to be. Sometimes I felt like the kid who started school later than all the other students, and had to work her brains out to catch up. I even had to learn how to pray.

Daniel's plea to God in Daniel 9:1–19 is a beautifully constructed prayer that is an example of how we should approach God. Daniel prayed with open and earnest repentance for his people. He knew that God is merciful and forgiving, and that He keeps His promises. He came to God with a humble and contrite heart. Daniel pleaded with God to return his people to their land. He was counting on God's promise through prophecy in Jeremiah 25:11. Note that Daniel *confesses* to God and then points out, "The Lord our God is merciful and forgiving, even though we have rebelled against him" (Daniel 9:9a, NIV).

Daniel was counting on God's mercy and forgiveness. Have you made a plea to God for forgiveness? Have you approached Him humbly and in full repentance, acknowledging His greatness? When you pray, do you first praise Him for His awesome love and spend time exalting his majesty?

When I first turned to God in prayer, I stammered

like a confused child. The words didn't want to come out, and I had to fight the temptation to choke them all back. Then I began to think about the magnitude of God's love. I marveled at the fact that I could turn to God and that He would not hate me or wag His finger at me. It doesn't get any better than that, and to think that He not only loved me no matter what I had done, but forgave me to boot. My heart was bursting with relief, and like a child praying for the first time, I kept saying, "Thank you, Jesus! Thank you, Lord! Thank you, thank you, thank you!"

I had to confess to Him all those awful things I had done and thought: the lack of regard for others, the pain and suffering I had caused my loved ones. I had to let it out and let it go. I had to lay my sin at the feet of Jesus and accept His forgiveness. Not until I did this was I able to move forward. Have you confessed your sins to God sincerely and without reserve, acknowledging the unending love God has for you regardless of your behavior?

In Colossians1:1–14, Paul reminds us of Christ's supreme sacrifice and the importance of praying for others. In his letter, he tells the Colossians that he and Timothy have not stopped praying for them and asking God to give them the knowledge to understand God's will. Paul reminds the Colossians of the purpose and supreme sacrifice of the Son of God: "For He has rescued us from the dominion of darkness and brought us into the kingdom of the Son He loves, in whom we have redemption, the forgiveness of sins" (Colossians 1:13–14, NIV).

Friend, do not forget what Jesus did for you! When you feel you have sinned so miserably that you can never pull out of the quicksand that you freely walked into, remember that God is merciful and forgiving. And God always keeps His promises!

Prayer of Gratefulness

Lord, I know that I have spent some years of my life going through the motions of being a Christian. I know that I have fallen so far from Your will that only a loving and merciful God would forgive and comfort me. Thank you, Lord, for drawing me to Your light and listening to my confession and plea for mercy. Thank you, Lord, for Your unconditional forgiveness! Amen.

Why Us?

I will have mercy on whom I have mercy,
and I will have compassion on whom I have
compassion.

—Romans 9–14b, NIV

My heart swells with intense gratitude when I consider how the Lord has taken mercy on my husband and me. He blesses us every day with a good marriage. I can say with absolute certainty that we have a fine and enduring relationship with each other because we have a fine and enduring relationship with Christ. At times, I have asked myself, "Why? How can our marriage be a good one? It started all wrong! We don't deserve it!" The answer is *mercy,* every minute of the day—God's mercy!

Nothing Joe and I ever did in our courtship was biblically sound. Our behavior flew in the face of God and was against the teachings of Christ. We hurt others, including our children. We lived a life of self-gratification with no regard for how our actions would affect others. And affect others they did. Even now, my conversations with my precious son sometimes end with, "You did this … You did that …" I know that deep in his heart he has not overcome the stigma and shame of having a notorious mother. I know that he loves me, and I continue to pray that he will someday come to terms with the past and its effect on his life. My daughter is a forgiving and sweet soul. She seems to have accepted God's grace in our lives and does not bring up old hurts. But I know that she too has issues because of my actions.

In his letter to the Ephesians, Paul gave instructions to children and parents:

> Children, obey your parents in the Lord for this is right. Honor your father and mother—which is the first commandment with a promise—that it may go well with you and that you may enjoy long life on earth. Fathers, do not exasperate your children; instead, bring them up in the way training and instruction of the Lord.

> —Ephesians 6:1–4, NIV

If you ask my children if I have ever exasperated them, they would burst out laughing and slap each other on the back. They would probably ask, "Which time?" Both of my children deeply love the Lord. They and their spouses are in ministry, and I will never be able to thank God enough for the love and mercy he has shown our family! In spite of the influence of my past behavior, God has a plan for all of us that transcends our upbringing.

Nathan, the prophet, confronted David with his sin of

adultery with Bathsheba, and also the murder of Uriah, in 2 Samuel 12:1–14. Later, David wrote Psalm 51:

> Have mercy on me, O God, according to Your unfailing love; according to Your great compassion blot out my transgressions. Wash away all my iniquity and cleanse me from my sin. For I know my transgressions, and my sin is always before me.
>
> —Psalm 51:1–3, NIV

> Create in me a pure heart, O God and renew a steadfast spirit within me. Do not cast me from Your presence or take Your Holy Spirit from me. Restore to me the joy of Your salvation and grant me a willing spirit, to sustain me.
>
> —Psalm 51:10–12, NIV

There is no question that David was overcome with pain and shame. Like David, I know that the pain and shame I felt choked me so that I could barely say the words, "Forgive me!" You might ask, "But Peg, how do you live with yourself? How do you live with the guilt?" In his old age, John wrote to reassure people who feel guilty and condemned.

> My dear children, I write this to you so that you will not sin. But if anybody does sin, we have One who speaks to the Father in our defense—Jesus Christ, the righteous One.

> He is the atoning sacrifice for our sins, and
> not only for ours but also for the sins of the
> whole world.

—1 John 2:1–2, NIV

Prayer for Humility

Father in Heaven, give me the humility to receive the intense love and mercy You have shown to my family and to me. Though I have done nothing to deserve Your forgiveness, You have seen fit to use me for Your glory. Only You can pull me from my sinful existence and set me on a straight path. Thank you, precious Lord! Amen.

Taking Responsibility

As for you, you were dead in your transgressions and sins, in which you used to live when you followed the ways of this world and the ruler of the kingdom of the air the spirit who is now at work in those who are disobedient. All of us also lived among them at one time, gratifying the cravings of our sinful nature and following its desires and thoughts. Like the rest, we were by nature objects of wrath. But because of His great love for us, God who is rich in mercy, made us alive with Christ even when we were dead in transgressions—it is by grace you have been saved.

—Ephesians 2:1–5, NIV

Some people try to *assign blame* for the things that happen to them. We often look at ourselves as the victims rather than the authors of our errors. We blame everyone and everything: parents, family, education, or lack of education. Some blame God, and some blame the devil. The fact is, our own behavior causes the troubles we encounter. I'm not talking about those things over which we have no control; I'm talking about what we do and the consequences of that behavior.

Some believe that for all the bad decisions we make, there is something or someone in our past or present who is responsible. An example is that of a man or a woman cheating on his or her spouse. According to this way of thinking, we must look at a person's history. If there is adultery, then that must be the root of the problem. Grandma did it, so then Mom did it, so then … Or the spouse wasn't attentive enough, didn't care how he or she looked. Then there is the "I was seduced" excuse. Aw c'mon! *Really?*

Of course there's, "The devil made me do it." Some people are quick to give Satan credit for what they themselves have done. I am always astounded when I hear this excuse from a professing Christian. Believer, the devil cannot *make* you do anything! In Romans 8:5–11, Paul points out the difference between those who are living sinfully and those who are living with the Holy Spirit dwelling in their hearts. Paul says that when we receive the Holy Spirit, we are no longer slaves to fear: "For you did not receive a spirit that makes you a slave again to fear, but you received the Spirit of Sonship. And by Him we cry, 'Abba, Father' (Romans 8:15, NIV).

James explains that through the trials and temptations in this life we have an opportunity to grow in character. He points out that God doesn't tempt us: "When tempted, no one should say, 'God is tempting me.' For God cannot be tempted by evil, nor does He tempt anyone; but each one is tempted when, by his own evil desire, he is dragged away and enticed (James 1:13–14, NIV). Did you catch the part in James that says, "by his *own* evil desire …"? God didn't *make* you sin; He only does the perfect good. "Every good and perfect thing is from above, coming down from the Father of the heavenly lights, Who does not change like shifting shadows" (James 1:17, NIV).

God is unchanging and everlasting! Reach out to Him when you feel tempted by evil desire. He is there for you to depend on, and He knows and cares about every situation you encounter! Sin is the cause of our evil desire. We can't lay the blame on anyone else. People who blame others for their mistakes are unwilling to take responsibility for their own actions and the consequences that follow. We can all cite something from our upbringing that formed the way we think and react, but recognizing that and dealing with it is the first step to changing our behavior. I was raised by a bitter man who belittled us. My mother chose to be defeated by him, but I do not have to let that unhappy part of my life determine how I am today. We don't have to be in bondage to our past. We don't have to imitate our parents' behavior. We don't have to carry the burden of our circumstances around like a scarlet letter.

God in His wisdom and mercy does not place His people in neat categories the way people do. It troubles me to hear a person say, "You are just like Uncle So-and-so. As long as you're alive, he'll never be dead." These things are said to children throughout their lives until they begin to believe it. How bleak our futures would be if we thought our destinies had been set by the actions of others. People who were raised believing statements like that can spend their entire lives trying to live down, or live up, to someone else's achievements. This is an unfair and impossible expectation. Praise God, we are under a new covenant!

> For this reason Christ is the mediator of a
> new covenant, that those who are called may
> receive the promised eternal inheritance—
> now that He has died as a ransom to set
> them free from the sins committed under
> the first covenant.
>
> —Hebrews 9:15, NIV

> This is the covenant I will make with them
> after that time, says the Lord. I will put My
> laws in their hearts, and I will write them
> on their minds." Then he adds: "Their sins
> and lawless acts I will remember no more.
>
> —Hebrews 10:16–17, NIV

Dear friend, you don't have to live in anyone's shadow. God made you a unique and special individual and gave you the choice to be the person He made you to be. Embrace that knowledge. Accept Christ into your heart, and let Him heal the past.

Prayer for Responsibility

Father, Your glory and splendor overwhelm my heart. Help me to take full responsibility for my behavior and not give in to the temptation to blame someone else. Help me always to remember that it is only by Your grace that my sins are forgiven. Amen.

Bringing It Up and Living It Down

Who is a God like You, Who pardons
sin and forgives the transgression of the
remnant of His inheritance? You do not stay
angry forever but delight to show mercy.

—Micah 7:18, NIV

It is typical for family members to bring up the most embarrassing things without batting an eye or giving a thought to how hurtful those memories are to us. They seem to disregard how much we have overcome and accomplished. Usually, our loved ones are not purposely being rude or cruel. But it feels like it, doesn't it?

People try to relive the past for various reasons: maybe their present is not so great, or maybe they'd like to remember when life seemed simpler, and maybe some just want to dredge up old hurts in order to justify themselves. I had a conversation with a relative that went like this:

"Remember when you dated so-and-so?"

"I can't believe you brought him up."

"But remember how the two of you …"

"I'd rather not."

"What did you ever see in him?"

"I was a kid, for crying out loud!"

"Yeah, but I still can't see what you saw in him. You're lucky to be alive. I was really worried about you then."

My relative was a person who couldn't shake off the past and move forward, and she was determined to make me relive the past with her. She ignored that I was in my forties, had raised a family, and had a fine and loving Christian husband. Sadly, many live every day in a perpetual circle. They are looking over their shoulders at the past while trying to walk forward. What happens if you walk forward while looking behind you? You are going to walk into something like a wall, or a post, or a person. "Ouch!" If I look into my past and punish myself over and over again, I'm ignoring God's forgiveness and disrespecting what He has done for me. If my heart is still broken over past mistakes, I can't be a true witness for God.

Is there someone in your life who tries to make you pay for your sins over and over? How precious is God's mercy, friend! How sweet is His love! The Lord doesn't dredge up our past and make us relive it. Without that gift, we would have no hope and no peace. Thank Jesus for His blessed assurance!

A Prayer for Peace

Precious Lord, thank You for Your love and mercy! I've lived a life of sin, for which I am ashamed. I know that through my true repentance before You, the one who shed Your blood for me, my sins have been forgiven. Help me to overcome my own crippling guilt so that I may serve You. As I read Your Word, give me understanding and peace. Amen.

Couple holding hands. Credit: kieferpix

Old Friends and New Friends

A friend loves at all times.

—Proverbs 17:17, NIV

A man of many companions may come to ruin, but there is a friend who sticks closer than a brother.

—Proverbs 18:24, NIV

Greater love has no one than this, that he lay down his life for his friends.

—John 15:13, NIV

If you asked a group of people to give their definition of *friend,* you'd get answers like "someone who is always there for you through the good times and the bad, loves you unconditionally no matter what you've done, and with whom you can share your deepest feelings without fearing judgment." There is only one friend who fits that description: His name is Jesus Christ. In His last words to Judas, the

Lord said, "Friend do what you came for" (Matthew 26:50a, NIV). Jesus knew how those words would profoundly affect His betrayer.

Recently, while I was in a gift shop that sold all kinds of fun things, I came across a coffee mug that said, "You'll always be my friend because you know too much." I nodded my head knowingly. Friends are confidants who know each other *very* well. Maybe your children grew up playing with their children. They know things about your past. Many old friends know more than your own family does about you. Like family members, old friends never forget. They will bring up stories that are better left forgotten. Old friends will look at you when you witness about the Lord with the "Oh, *really?*" look. They will demand an explanation, and rightly so. They want to know why you did *that* but now are doing *this.* And they often have a very hard time believing their ears. The biggest challenge for a reformed person is to witness to family and old friends. Should we leave behind old friends and start afresh with new ones? Jesus said, "Go into all the world and preach the good news to all creation" (Mark 16:15, NIV).

Now is your chance to witness to friends. It should be exciting to approach an old friend who knows all about you and say, "I've changed through the grace of Jesus Christ." But people might say things like "Yes, I remember that you went to church with your first husband. We know how that worked out. What makes this time different?" If you are unprepared, shame and embarrassment can overwhelm you. The amount of preparation we do before approaching someone can make a difference in whether or not that person accepts what we have to say. Preparation begins with *prayer.*

There is no point in trying to move forward without first bringing the situation before the Lord. Bring your feelings of shame and inadequacy to Him. When I pray, I present the different scenarios that are going through my mind. I imagine God as a sounding board, and I rely on Him to encourage me through the Holy Spirit. I don't want to face any situation without God's blessing. I like to practice. This may seem strange to some, but for me, practicing what I'm going to say out loud is a help. What if old friends won't accept the gospel? What if they scoff and shun you? In Luke 9:1–6, Jesus sent out the twelve disciples with strict instructions: "If people do not welcome you, shake the dust off your feet when you leave their town, as a testimony against them" (Luke 9:5, NIV). This doesn't mean to forget about them or to stop praying for them. Everyone fears the unknown. It may not be easy to accept that someone they have known for years has changed and has a new message for them. Give your friends time to think about what you've said. I have witnessed to old friends who scoffed at me but then years later were led to Christ by someone else. We were able to reconnect, but this time through a relationship bonded in Christ.

When Jesus began teaching the people in Nazareth, whom He had known all his life, they were offended. Does that surprise you? Suppose someone you have known all your life reappears in town and claims to be the Savior … hmm. "And they took offense at Him. But Jesus said to them, 'Only in his hometown and in his own house is a prophet without honor'" (Matthew 13:57, NIV).

Jesus' family had another whole set of issues to deal with: "For even His own brothers did not believe Him"

(John 7:5, NIV). Jesus had done nothing wrong. He hadn't lived a sinful life and had nothing in his past that pointed to shame, yet family and old friends rejected Him. Why? Old acquaintances may have been too stunned to believe that this kid they had grown up with was the Son of God.

What about those *new* friends? You know who I mean—Christian friends. What do they know about you? Chances are they know little or nothing about your past. A good friend shouldn't want to know all the sordid details of your unsaved past. But what if your new friend hears something about you that you don't want to talk about? It isn't necessary to give details of your sinful past, and Christian friends should not expect an explanation. "For all have sinned and fall short of the glory of God, and are justified freely by His grace through the redemption that came by Christ Jesus" (Romans 3:23–24, NIV).

When witnessing to others, praying specifically for discernment is paramount. Some people don't need or want to hear all the details. Your Christian friends should not judge you for past mistakes, but it is important to be forthright about them. It is enough to be honest without giving details, and it is enough that Jesus Christ forgives you.

You may meet someone who *needs* to hear about God's forgiveness. You may have to share more with that person than you might with someone else. The Holy Spirit at times compels me to share how merciful God has been to me. There are people who are suffering deeply from shame and need to hear how He can change you and use you for His glory.

I recently had a frank and honest conversation with a woman who had made the same types of mistakes that I had made and feared what others would think and say about her. I could feel her embarrassment, and my heart broke for her. When I shared with her what I had been through, and that I too had to pray and trust that God had forgiven me, I could see the relief flood her face. This was one of those times when a beloved sister in Christ was struggling and needed to know there was someone she could relate to.

My church family members are precious. Their love and respect are very important to me. Don't underestimate the power of God's people agreeing in prayer. Take your needs to them. They are your sisters and brothers, your moms and dads, your grandmas and grandpas. Their children are your nieces and nephews. Remember that they need your love and support as much as you need theirs. Keep them dear to your heart, and hold them up in prayer!

Prayer for Friends

Father, I love my friends. I love that You have joined me with other people so that I have someone to relate to and share with. I know that old friends may have a hard time believing that I really have changed, and I know that it may take the rest of my life to convince them that I'm not the person I was before. Give me discernment, and let me be an example for others and prove to them that You do change the heart. Amen.

Overcoming Unwanted Reminders

And now, dear children, continue in Him, so that when He appears we may be confident and unashamed before Him at His coming.

—1 John 2:28, NIV

What is it that makes you think of the past? Is it the sight of something or someone? Is it a song that you hear on the radio? Is it the smell of someone's cologne? Is it the feel of a certain fabric against your skin?

When I was growing up in California, every summer we camped in Yosemite National Park. Dad rented a cabin consisting of cinder block walls and a canvas top and front. There was also a patio area with a small wood-burning stove for cooking. The pleasant smells of canvas, wet bathing suits, wood burning in the stove, pine trees, and soap are the most endearing memories of my childhood. We played in the icy water of the Merced River, and every night, Mom would stand us up in a wash tub and scrub us down with soap. After we were tucked into our cots, we listened wide-eyed for the sound of bears scavenging through the camp trash cans. Most of us have memories like our Yosemite trip. Those sights and smells will take us right back to that time.

When I was six weeks pregnant with my first baby, I suffered from intense nausea, like most first-time mothers. Relatives who lived in the country asked us to house-sit while they were away. Naturally, I jumped at the chance to spend time in the country. One night, I was awakened by the sound of howling dogs. As I sat up in bed, rubbing my eyes and trying to understand what was happening, Shelby, a German shepherd, charged through the doggy door, bounded into the bedroom, and jumped onto the middle of the bed. Instantly, the smell of skunk hit me. Shelby had been sprayed in the face by a skunk and was rubbing his burning eyes all over me and the bed! My stomach lurched and roiled like it never had before. That was over forty years ago, and to this day, whenever I smell skunk, I am overcome with morning sickness!

I have always been sensitive to smells. There is a specific perfume that jolts my memory back to a man I dated years before I met Joe. He bought that scent for me as a gift, and I wore it every time we went out. For a long time, when I was in public and got a whiff of that perfume, the smell took me right back to thoughts of him. First I remembered romantic, starlit evenings and dancing. Then I remembered sitting in a restaurant staring at my plate because if I looked up, he would accuse me of looking at other men. I remembered not being allowed to watch certain shows on TV because he would accuse me of lusting after some TV character. I remembered keeping my mouth shut when we were with his friends because if I spoke to them, he thought I was flirting. There comes a time when those so-called good memories are overshadowed by the bad.

I strive to move forward in God's plan for me. I am resolved, with the Lord's help, to put my past behind me. Writing about it is the closest I've come to remembering those years. As a Christian, I strive to live in the here and now. I got rid of the reminders. I tossed out that perfume. I didn't give it away; I threw it in the trash because I did not want to run into the person I had given it to and smell it on her. I avoided listening to our special song until hearing it no longer pulled up old memories. I threw away that favorite dress—you know, the one that flowed so beautifully around me when I twirled. I dumped it instead of giving it away because I didn't want to see it again. The jewelry and other gifts had to go. If someone persisted in talking about that part of my past, I politely told him or her to stop. If the chatter continued, I stopped associating with that person until the message got through. John stressed that we should not allow ungodly people to influence us: "Dear children, do not let anyone lead you astray. He who does what is right is righteous, just as He is righteous" (1 John 3:7, NIV).

"But Peg," you might say, "I had children with *him.*" I understand. I have been a single mother of two, so I know firsthand what it is like to deal with an ex-husband. I realized he was going to be in my life, by association, forever. I learned to live with it. Your children love their father as much as they love you, and rightly so. Keep in mind that your children aren't objects. They are gifts from God. They are a living, breathing part of you and a living, breathing part of their father.

Peggy Clevenger

Prayer for Overcoming Reminders

Sweet Jesus, there is no experience or memory that can compare with being Your child. There is no love from another person that can run as deeply and be as endearing as the abiding love You have for me. Earthly relationships begin and end, but You are everlasting. Help me to overcome memories that take me back to a life I have left behind, so that I may serve You. Amen.

Crying woman in monochrome Credit: Antonuk

Dealing with Guilt

> Here is a trustworthy saying that deserves
> full acceptance: Christ Jesus came into the
> world to save sinners—of whom I am the
> worst.
>
> —1 Timothy 1:15, NIV

As a young woman, I lived a disgusting life of sin. I call that time "the dark years," and the saddest part of all is that I dragged my children through it with me. There are times when guilt and shame can become crippling and cause intense depression. If not for the precious love and forgiveness of Christ, I would have taken my own life long ago.

Before his conversion on the road to Damascus, Saul was a merciless persecutor of Christians. He was a major participant at the stoning of Stephen:

> At this they covered their ears, and yelling
> at the top of their voices, they all rushed at
> him, dragged him out of the city and began
> to stone him. Meanwhile, the witnesses laid

their clothes at the feet of a young man named Saul.

—Acts 7:57–58, NIV

He did everything in his power to destroy the church:

But Saul began to destroy the church. Going from house to house he dragged off men and women and put them in prison.

—Acts 8:3, NIV

He was prepared to do whatever it took to stop the flow of Good News:

Meanwhile, Saul was still breathing out murderous threats against the Lord's disciples. He went to the high priest and asked him for letters to the synagogues in Damascus, so that if he found any there who belonged to the Way, whether men or women, he might take them as prisoners to Jerusalem.

—Acts 9-1–2, NIV

His conversion is described in Acts:

> He fell to the ground and heard a voice say to him, "Saul, Saul, why do you persecute Me?"

> —Acts 9:4, NIV

Saul changed drastically. During his ministry, he began to use the Greek version of his name, Paul. He became a renowned missionary to the Gentiles. Yet he made a telling statement in 2 Corinthians:

> To keep me from becoming conceited because of these surpassingly great revelations, there was given me a thorn in my flesh, a messenger of Satan to torment me. Three times I pleaded with the Lord to take it away from me. But He said to me, "My grace is sufficient for you, for My power is made perfect in weakness."

> —2 Corinthians 12:7–9a, NIV

Many have speculated on exactly what Paul's "thorn" was. Was it a physical illness? Was it a crippled limb? I have a theory that the apostle Paul's thorn was the pain of guilt. Whether Paul's thorn was physical or emotional, it bothered him enough that he pleaded with God three times to take it away. When I read this passage, I'm compelled to fall on my face before God! There were times when bouts of oppressive guilt caused me deep despair until I could hardly hold my head up.

In his letter to the Philippians, Paul said:

> Brothers, I do not consider myself yet to have taken hold of it. But one thing I do: Forgetting what is behind and straining toward what is ahead, I press on toward the goal to win the prize for which God has called me heavenward in Christ Jesus.
>
> —Philippians 3:13–14, NIV

Friend, Paul put a lot of bad behavior behind him in order to press on for Jesus. And so can we! It is only by the grace of God that I have been able to overcome episodes of guilt and self-loathing. I don't even try to stop the tears of gratitude, knowing that He has seen my torment and cares how I feel. Like Paul, I depend on God's grace, so that I can press on toward the goal!

A Prayer to Overcome Crippling Guilt

Father, like Paul, I too have a thorn in my flesh. I have an affliction of guilt that paralyzes me at times, rendering me ineffectual. The knowledge that You have forgiven me keeps me striving to overcome these intense feelings of guilt. Thank you for reminding me that through Your grace I am made stronger! Amen.

Forgive and Be Forgiven

Therefore, if you are offering your gift at the
altar and there remember that your brother
has something against you, leave your gift
there in front of the altar. First go and be
reconciled to your brother; then come and
offer your gift.

—Matthew 5:23–24, NIV

Asking forgiveness is complicated. It involves more
than just saying, "I'm sorry." You have to mean what you
say, humbly feel what you say, and convey the words in a
convincing way, without saying too much or too little. You
also must be prepared for the possibility that the offended
party might not forgive you. If these words make you want
to run and hide, join the crowd.

When I was a young mother, my four-year-old daughter
Erin and her four-year-old male cousin often played together.
Erin was a tiny child, but he was a big boy who outweighed
her by about five pounds. One day, while I was visiting
with the boy's mother, we heard screams coming from the

playroom. Jumping up, we found Erin holding her tummy. She pointed at her big cousin and cried, "He hit me!"

His mother, clearly angry, yelled, "You tell her you're sorry right now!"

He poked out his bottom lip in an offended pout and said, "Sorry."

I still remember how incensed I was that he was getting away with such a lame apology! How dare that giant child attack my precious little darling? How could his mother think that he could really mean he was sorry? Couldn't she see he had taken unfair advantage of the difference in their sizes? Sometimes, even a *humble* apology can seem like too little too late. Thankfully, the Lord sees into our hearts and knows how sincere we are.

When you apologize to someone, just about anything can happen: the person can throw his or her arms around you in joyful tears of reconciliation, turn and walk away without a word, or even get in your face and curse you. How do you know when and how you should apologize? Go to your pastor or spiritual advisor for counsel. I can't stress enough the importance of asking the Holy Spirit to give you discernment as to whether the apology should be face to face, whether you should send a note, or whether to apologize at all. Remember too that this might be a situation that warrants bringing your pastor along. Keep in mind that your apology is for the offended person's gratification, not to make you feel better at the expense of causing someone else more pain. A friend once told me that a relative came to her after church one day and said, "God has impressed upon me to apologize for my rudeness to you. Just because I don't like you doesn't give me an excuse to be cruel!" Needless to say, my friend was flabbergasted.

One day, four of us at work were sitting around a table during our break talking about the story of Ruth and Boaz. One of the ladies made a statement that so astonished me that I blurted out, "You're totally wrong about that!" She turned red in the face, and everyone got up and walked out of the room in silence. That night, I couldn't sleep for the guilt I felt! I believe everyone is entitled to an opinion, and it's wrong to make a person feel invalidated just because I don't agree. Now I had done that very thing! My eyes are smarting in shame right now at the memory of what I said. The next day, I apologized to her in front of the other two ladies. Not only did I owe her an apology, but I needed to do it in front of those who witnessed the offense.

We can offend a person so deeply and with so many repercussions that a face to face confrontation is out of the question. Even a note might be a bad idea because what you write down goes on record. Again, seek the counsel of your pastor or spiritual advisor and pray!

Now that we've established the importance of apologizing to people, what about the other side of that street? Are you a forgiving person? Are you a person who can forgive some offenses but not others? Are some people easier to forgive because you like them better? Do the offenders have to apologize before you will forgive them in your heart?

Sometimes we are "righteously" offended. A Christian friend once told me about a woman she had been introduced to (I'll call her Carol). Carol had some negative history. She had left her husband for another man. Now, years later, Carol is beginning a relationship with a new man. They are attending church together and are discussing marriage. Carol and her first husband had also been avid churchgoers, but she had made some very bad decisions and was trying to make a fresh start. My friend, who knew about Carol's past, already had a negative attitude toward her when they were introduced. Carol talked to my friend about what the Lord had done for her in the past, and how He was working in her life. My friend said that throughout the conversation, she kept thinking, "How dare you talk about God's goodness to you when I know all about what you have done!" She kept her mouth shut while she seethed inside. I'm sure that Carol sensed the negative attitude; who wouldn't?

I asked my friend, "Don't you think that Carol is sorry for her mistakes?"

Her reply was, "I didn't see any evidence of it!"

I've since wondered exactly what kind of "evidence" my friend was looking for. Did she expect Carol to weep in misery over having disappointed her husband, God, or the church? Did she expect a personal apology? Was Carol supposed to flush with shame at being in the presence of such a good Christian woman?

My friend's reaction was a typical example of how many people would respond to the same situation. As human beings, we can't see into the hearts and minds of others. So how are we to determine the sincerity of another? We try to judge by watching their behavior, but in the back of our minds, there is that twinge of doubt and mistrust.

In all things, we should behave in a Christ-like manner. Is it up to us to determine whether or not someone has repented, or should we leave that up to God? Are we to have righteous indignation toward others who have slipped?

Why can't we just let God handle it? If I focus on my own behavior and my own relationship with God, then I don't have time to judge someone else. Do I have the right to be self-righteous toward others who have made mistakes that I may not have made? That kind of attitude tends to come back to roost. What did Jesus say?

> To some who were confident of their own righteousness and looked down on everyone else, Jesus told this parable: "Two men went up to the temple to pray, one a Pharisee and the other a tax collector. The Pharisee stood by himself and prayed: 'God, I thank You that I am not like other people—robbers, evildoers, adulterers—or even like this tax collector. I fast twice a week and give a tenth of all I get.' "But the tax collector stood at a distance. He would not even look up to heaven, but beat his breast and said, 'God, have mercy on me, a sinner.' "I tell you that this man, rather than the other, went home justified before God. For all those who exalt themselves will be humbled, and those who humble themselves will be exalted."

> —Luke 18:9–14, NIV

I have been guilty of carrying anger and offense around inside, allowing them to fester, and revealing my feelings with something as simple as a look. The only thing I gained from this was a migraine. I allowed my own stubborn pride to make me sick while the offender was going along his merry way, not even giving me a thought.

When I refuse to forgive, I am placing myself in bondage to my own emotions and disobeying Christ. Jesus put the need to forgive into perspective: "For if you forgive men when they sin against you, your heavenly Father will also forgive you. But if you do not forgive men their sins, your Father will not forgive your sins" (Matthew 6:14–15, NIV). Paul explained how to live as children of light: "Be kind and compassionate to one another, forgiving each other just as in Christ God forgave you" (Ephesians 4:32, NIV).

You remember the golden rule, don't you? "So in everything, do to others what you would have them do to you, for this sums up the Law of the Prophets" (Matthew 7:12, NIV). Fifty years ago, when I was in the fourth grade, a plaque with those words printed on it hung on the wall in our public school room. Since the day the Savior uttered them, they've been an example of a perfect attitude and the only godly way to live. This has been true since the beginning, and it will hold true throughout eternity.

A Prayer for a Heart of Forgiveness

Father, I have offended people so deeply that I can't imagine them ever forgiving me. I want those I have hurt to know how truly sorry I am, but I need the discernment of the Holy Spirit to know how to apologize. I realize, too, that there are those I may never be able to confront, and I pray that You will witness to their hearts and give them peace.

Lord, soften my heart toward others who have offended me. Remind me how important it is to obey You and be a forgiving person for my own spiritual peace. Help me to be more like You. Amen.

Woman feet running on road. Credit: Dmitrii Kotin

Moving Forward for God

He put a new song in my mouth, a hymn of
praise to our God. Many will see and fear
and put their trust in the Lord.

—Psalm 40:3, NIV

I am as directionally challenged as anyone can be; I am
notorious for getting lost. I've heard it said that people raised
on the coast, as I was, often have this problem. Without
an ocean to navigate by, I have no clue in which direction
I'm going. Take me away from the coast, and I become
instantly turned around. All hills and valleys look the same
to me. All rivers, lakes, and ponds seem the same. And
don't get me started on tract homes! You know, where all
the houses are built from one or two patterns and they're
all grouped together. The streets wind round and round
and round … You get the idea. Remember back before cell
phones? I would somehow get turned around and have to
drive for miles before finding a pay phone. Do those even
exist anymore? Something in my head says, "This looks like
a way to go—I'll go this way!" Once I realize I've made a
wrong turn, I become paralyzed with confusion. Then panic

sets in. I start sweating, gasping for air, and crying copious tears. I'm hyperventilating just at the thought!

Changing a lifestyle can cause the same dazed and fearful reaction. Guilt over an unsavory past can paralyze a person's ability to move forward. Satan uses guilt to put ideas into our heads. When I say, "I want to do a work for God," he says, "Work? What kind of work can you do? Everyone is staring at you, pointing, whispering to each other 'Pssst— We don't want her in our group, I'll tell you why later.'" Years ago, I was acquainted with a couple who, through the grace of God, have learned to deal with guilt and shame. They spent most of their married lives dealing drugs and lived quite comfortably in an upscale neighborhood. They both had reputable jobs and the ability to hide their illegal activities from the authorities. The husband became quite ill, and the prognosis was very bad. During this stressful time of intense pain and uncertainty, they were led to Christ. They began attending church, became dedicated to the work of the Lord, and got completely out of the drug business. They are an inspiring example of how people who turn to Christ can change their lives.

During a recent visit with this man and his wife, I remarked on how much I enjoyed being around them because of their open and forthright love for Jesus. I'll never forget how red the man's face became as he said quietly, "Well, we try the best we can." I knew in my heart that he was feeling that old embarrassment at talking to someone who knew about his past.

I said, "Hang in there! We are all in this thing together, and the Lord sees our hearts." Friend, let me tell you something with absolute certainty: God wants you to move forward for His glory. He knows all our past. But remember: because He has forgiven, He has forgotten. Scripture says, "Their sins and lawless acts I will remember no more" (Hebrews 10:16–17).

One of the most inspiring accounts of a person changing her life and becoming a child of God is told in the book of Joshua. Rahab, the prostitute, wasn't tucked away in some back alley. She lived on the wall of Jericho. Everyone in town knew who and what she was. When she realized that the God of Israel was the only real and true God, she made a decision to completely turn her life around. She was willing to risk death to defend God's people. She told the spies: "When we heard of it, our hearts melted and everyone's courage failed because of you, for the Lord your God is God in heaven above and on the earth below" (Joshua 2:11, NIV). She wanted one thing in return: a second chance, for herself and her loved ones.

> Now then, please swear to me by the Lord that you will show kindness to my family, because I have shown kindness to you. Give me a sure sign that you will spare the lives of my father and mother, my brothers and sister, and all who belong to them, and that you will save us from death.
>
> —Joshua 2:12–13, NIV

What eventually happened to Rahab?

> Joshua said to the two men who had spied out the land, "Go into the prostitute's house

and bring her out and all who belong to her,
in accordance with your oath to her. So the
young men who had done the spying went
in and brought out Rahab, her father and
mother and brothers and all who belonged
to her. They brought out her entire family
and put them in a place outside the camp
of Israel.

—Joshua 6:22, 23 NIV

She and her entire family were saved! She made a decision to change, and as a result, she changed the lives of everyone she loved! In James, her righteous behavior was noted right along with Abraham's! That's pretty impressive, don't you think?

In the same way, was not even Rahab the
prostitute considered righteous for what she
did when she gave lodging to the spies and
sent them off in a different direction?

—James 2:25 NIV

In Hebrews, we read:

By faith the prostitute Rahab, because she
welcomed the spies, was not killed with
those who were disobedient.

—Hebrews 11:31, NIV

Rahab is noted in Matthew 1:5 as being a direct ancestor of Christ. She was a woman who made a decision to change her life, and move forward for God. She didn't let her reputation stop her or determine her future. She didn't let fear of what others might think deter her. Friend, you don't have to let your past stop you from moving forward for God. He has a work for you, and it's up to you to make the choice to obey His calling in your life. When you made the decision to turn away from a sinful life and obey the will of God, you took on a new set of obstacles, but no obstacle is too hard or too high for God to overcome! Place yourself in His hands, stay in constant prayer, study His word, and surround yourself with others of like mind.

The Lord will guide you through each day. All you have to do is ask Him and place yourself at His feet. He loves you, He forgives you, He has forgotten your sin, and He is looking forward to seeing you face to face.

Prayer for the Future

Father in Heaven, I don't know how much time I have left on this earth. What I do know is that I want to spend it doing a work for You. I can only face the future knowing that You are here to guide me. With Your guidance, I'll get through this life and someday meet You in person. Oh, how glorious that day will be! Amen and amen.

Printed in the United States
By Bookmasters